T·R·U·E
T·E·A·M

Make your business a game where every player wins

Tony Melvin & Mikel Lindsaar

T.R.U.E T.E.A.M

Published by

MetaPulse.com

Contents

Winning

Michael Jordan wiped the sweat from his forehead. The 20-second timeout provided a much needed rest. His team, the Chicago Bulls, were trailing 2 points behind the Utah Jazz. Whoever won this game would win the 1998 NBA Championship. The stakes were high as it would be championship number six for both Jordan and the Bulls, if he and his team could pull it off. It was also rumored, at the time, that Jordan intended to retire from basketball at the end of the season, making this his final game.

With only 59 seconds left, Jordan approached the free throw line. He sank both free throw shots, tying the score at 83. Now the Jazz had possession. To the Bull's dismay, seconds later, the Jazz scored an impressive 3-pointer and another timeout was called.

With 41 seconds left, the Jazz were ahead 86 to 83.

The Bulls had possession. Long-time Jordan teammate Scottie Pippen passed the ball to Jordan, who artfully navigated through the Jazz defense, claiming a 2-point basket. The score had closed to a 1-point gap with the Bulls behind at 85.

Now the Jazz had possession with 37 seconds left on the clock.

As the Jazz team tried to break the Bulls defense, Jordan stole the ball from Jazz's star player Karl Malone. With 17 seconds to go, the Bulls were in position at the Jazz end of the court. Jordan was just outside the 3-point line, casually dribbling the ball, looking for an opening. He attacked, faked right, stopped short, and launched straight up in the air, letting the ball fly from just inside the 3-point line. As Jordan touched down, the ball went through the ring, putting the Bulls 1 point ahead with 5 seconds left in the game.

The Jazz call another timeout. When they returned to the court, their final shot failed to make it through the ring. Michael Jordan and the Bulls won their sixth NBA Title.

Some 22 years earlier, another team set out to make history in a different sport entirely. The 24 Hours of Le Mans is an endurance-focused car race held annually near the town of Le Mans, France. It is the oldest active endurance racing event. It differs from usual car races, where the winner is determined by minimum time over a fixed distance; the 24 Hours of Le Mans is won by the car that covers the greatest distance in 24 hours.

In the year of 1966, the race had been dominated for the most part over the past decade by one car maker—Ferrari. Several years earlier, in 1963, Lee Iacocca, then Vice President of Ford Motor Company, convinced Henry Ford II to buy Ferrari as a means of boosting sales. Ferrari's founder and owner, Enzo Ferrari, used the Ford offer to secure a more lucrative deal with Fiat, which also allowed him to retain ownership of the Ferrari Racing Team.

Furious by rejection and supposed insults, Iacooca and Ford decided to build their own racing team to compete with Ferrari and win the coveted 24 Hours of Le Mans. For the task, Iacocca hired American car builder and former Le Mans winner Carroll Shelby.

Shelby's team designed and built the Ford GT Mustang, which, aside from taking first, second and third place in the 24 hours of Le Mans of 1966, went on to win in 67, 68, and 69. Furthermore, the GT Mustang became the highest selling Ford vehicle. To this day, it is the longest-produced Ford car.

To yet another sport—women's tennis. Venus Williams was only 14 years old when she went up against the world number 2 player. Although she lost that game, halfway through, she was winning. And this was her first professional match. Venus and her sister Serena went on to become the most successful women's double pairs of all time. Venus ranks second in all-time career prize money, and guess who is number one? Her sister Serena.

There are countless examples of stellar achievements, and while we could go on, let's get to the crux of this book and ask a pertinent question: What made these teams great?

Yes, athletic skills played a part, as did experience, just like it does with any endeavor. But Michael Jordan could not win the championship alone, just as Carroll Shelby could not build a car alone, and the Williams twins didn't become great by themselves.

There will always be a star who is out in front of the public eye, but they only ever succeed when surrounded by a team. Someone has to clean the lockers, order the uniforms, manage the money, service the car, coach the players, schedule travel, and do all the other unforeseen tasks. Even one-player sports like tennis need a team to win.

And that's our first message: *Winning takes a team.*

But not just any team. Winning takes a *true team.*

We're going to show you how to build one, and we'll provide you with the tools to do so.

Ready to win?

Let's start with the blueprint of a True Team.

A True Team

The word *team* can be loosely defined as a group of two or more people working together. But winning takes much more than that.

Winning takes a radically focused, totally engaged, never-give-up, kind of team. But how do you build such a team? How do you find the real players? How do you keep them radically focused and totally committed? Is it even possible?

Yes, it is possible and in this book we'll show you how.

When building anything, having a blueprint saves a lot of time and energy, because then you know what you are building.

The following nine chapters of this book explain the blueprint of a True Team and the tools you can use to build such a Team. In the final chapter we'll introduce the Growth League, which is the playground where you can test the performance of your Team in the real world and see if you've got what it takes to win. More on that later.

For now, let's start with the most important part—*the foundation.*

A True Team is a...

Truly (to the fullest degree; genuinely or properly, in actual fact and without doubt)

Radical (characterized by independence of or departure from tradition; innovative or unorthodox)

Unrelenting (not yielding in strength, severity, or determination)

Enterprise

of

<u>T</u>otally (completely; absolutely)
<u>E</u>ngaged (pledge oneself to do something)
<u>A</u>ligned (put into correct or appropriate relative positions)
<u>M</u>embers.

From now on, when we mention *Team,* we'll do so with a capital T. This is to differentiate between the common use of the word. When we use the word Team, we mean a *True Team,* one with all of the above mentioned attributes.

As a final comment on the concept of Team, it's worth noting that it comes from the Latin word *ducere,* "to lead," which in its most basic sense means *to cause a person to go forward.*

Therefore, the final attribute of a True Team is that each member in it causes all other members to move forward; to move in the same direction toward an objective or goal. This further tells you that those who don't move the Team forward or who hinder the Team in some way are not True Team members.

Those who help move the Team forward, who are totally engaged and aligned, are called *players.*

Those who hinder, or demonstrate disengagement or unalignment, are *spectators.*

Needless to say, we want a Team of *players.*

That's achieved by knowing and following the True Team Blueprint, which is composed of 9 Building Blocks. Let's start with Building Block #1: *There has to be a reason to play.*

Building Block 1:

There Has to Be a Reason to Play

Why do elite athletes push themselves beyond limits? Why are world records continually beaten? What possesses fans to brave miserable weather, endure the wait of long queues, and suffer the cost of pricey tickets?

The answer is this: they all want to win. The players, the managers, and the fans all want to win. They have a common purpose to be the best in their field.

In sports, the common purpose is inherent in the competition and the game. Everyone knows how to win. The structure and purposes are well defined and known. That's why people love sports, because they all share a common purpose. They all have a reason to play or to support the players.

Business is also a game.

While you might not have fanatical fans packing a stadium to see you perform (yet!), or national media coverage of your daily activities, business still has all the elements of a game, and winning at business can be just as thrilling as any sports game. I bet you can think of some businesses that have achieved a massive following and have stadiums full of fans at their conferences and events.

The first element of a Team is having a common purpose. It doesn't need to be a "change the world" kind of thing, but it does need to be clear, concise, and motivating. And above all, it must be known by every player on your Team.

This is the magnet that attracts like-minded people and keeps them together, working through thick and thin and overcoming the challenges towards the common goal. It gives the Team members a focus they can align with and a reason to engage.

So the first step is to answer this question:

*Why are you playing the game of
[your business name]?*

Ensure you write in a way that will attract and motivate other players. Don't make this a self-centered purpose such as "to build a business I can sell for a billion dollars" or "to create passive income," as that will not attract great players to your Team. Think about how passionate you would be if the sole purpose of your job was to help your boss retire early?

The reason to play must be genuine, it must come from the heart, it must be something you are passionate about, it should get you excited, and just as important, it should get your Team excited.

While there is nothing wrong with having the goal to sell a business for a billion dollars, such a goal is usually achieved as a side effect of the founders having an unrelenting desire to make a difference and to solve a major problem in society. It's that unrelenting desire that attracts others with the same purpose. That is when a True Team is born.

So go ahead and answer the question above and make it broadly known. Post it in a place where all can see. Share it with every Team member. Remind your Team regularly of the reason why you are playing the game. Once you've done the above, you're ready for the next Building Block: *Every player has a position.*

Building Block 2:

Every Player Has a Position

One of the first elements that permits a Team to work together in harmony is that *every player has a position.*

In sports such as football, soccer, and basketball, there are positions that attack (score goals) and positions that defend. If a defender on the team kept trying to attack and score goals, that player would leave their defense weak. No matter how skilled the individual player is, the entire team would suffer. One slip of the ball that gives the opposing team possession could lose the game.

As an extreme example, imagine a goalie in a soccer game who tried to attack every time they got the ball. Instead of passing it to an attacker on their team, they took it upon themselves and dribbled it toward the opposing goal to try to score. In doing so, they leave their team's goal wide open. In soccer, nobody but the goalie can use their hands to control the ball. Such a goalie puts their team at a major disadvantage and would eventually lose the game.

This of course never happens in sports, why? Because before walking onto the field, all the players are given positions, they know the purpose and function of their role, they know the rules, they also know the position and functions of the other players. But often, in business, we hire new employees and let them walk on the field without this basic knowledge. We don't give them a position. Perhaps they know some of the rules and a little of what they are meant to do, but in many cases, they are like the attack-goalie, leaving their position open, trying to achieve something and discovering the rules of the game by trial and error. Most figure out their position on the team through experience.

This is a slow and inefficient way to build a True Team. There's a much better way. It requires following 3 steps:

1. Design Your Playing Field
2. Add the Existing Players
3. Identify the Missing Players

Step 1: Design Your Playing Field

The first step is to design your playing field. What roles are needed to win at your game?

While all businesses are different, no matter their size, they all have a very definite set of functions that include the following:

1. Management
2. Recruitment or Team Building
3. Promotion & Marketing
4. Sales
5. Accounting
6. Quality Control
7. Business Development
8. Making a Product or Delivering a Service

The above list is not a playing field. We need to turn this into a diagram or a map of the business so every player can easily see where they fit. Here's an example:

This is often called an *organizational chart* or *organizational structure*. We prefer to call it a Team Chart.

Step 2: Add the Existing Players

The next step is to add all of the existing players to your Team Chart.

While doing this, you may discover some players have more than one position. This is often the case with fledging and growing businesses. If you are the business founder, you may find yourself splattered all over the Team Chart. Now you know why it's hard to get everything done–you are playing more than one position!

The good news is, by doing the above actions, you are taking your first few steps toward reducing your workload.

The most important thing to do at this stage is to note it all down. As the owner, if you are handling management, sales, marketing, service, and delivery, then your name should go onto the Team Chart five times with each role you fill. If your receptionist is also the accounts receivable manager and the office manager, then they would be on the Team Chart three times.

Adding all the players to your Team Chart allows you to immediately see who is overloaded with work and what functions in your organization are not likely getting done.

Step 3: Identify the Missing Positions

It's also vital to identify the missing positions in your Team. These are roles that are needed but nobody has been hired to do. It's best practice to put every function or role on your Team Chart, even if no one is currently doing that function, as this makes it plainly obvious to all other players that nobody is there. It also provides a roadmap for recruitment. You'll discover that the duties of those missing positions are the ones that often end up on your plate.

Become Team-Centric

Your Team Chart is the most vital tool in your organization. This may seem like an overstatement, but consider this: How effective would a sports team be if all the players walked out on the field without the slightest clue of their position and started to play, randomly defending or attacking? The result would be chaos. By having a clear and concise Team Chart, *every player knows their position.*

How to Create Your Team Chart

The fastest way to create a Team Chart is with good ol' pen and paper. Take a big sheet of paper or start with a few pieces of paper taped together and sketch it out and stick it on the wall. Take a photo and share it with the Team. Later, you can use a spreadsheet or create your Team Chart in MetaPulse.com (which is free to do).

The key is to create your Team Chart as soon as possible and to share this vital tool with your entire Team, so they know their position as a player in the game.

Case Studies

We asked several clients who have successfully implemented this Building Block about the challenges they faced and what difference it made in their business. Here's what they had to say.

CASE STUDY #1: Company Name Withheld, approximately 1,800 employees

Q. Tell us about your Team Chart.

We've always had one, even when we were just a small group. Now we're over 1800 staff. Having a Team Chart becomes critical as you don't know who is doing what without that.

When you're a startup, you do everything. As you grow, you're constantly handing over functions, giving them to someone else. Having the Team Chart is critical so those functions can be identified and assigned to somebody.

You've got to have each function on it so you can show the person where they sit in relation to other people in the company, what their lines of authority are, and what their responsibilities are. Then you can tell them, "Now go for it!"

Q. How did it benefit your company and growth?

It gave us stability for one. It created faster movement of things within the company and enabled us to help our customers faster and to get things done quicker. It helped facilitate hyper growth.

Q. What challenges did you face implementing your Team Chart?

We had several iterations of it. The challenge had to do with figuring out the best way to achieve a particular result and figuring out all the sub-activities necessary to achieve it. We had to work those out and then adjust the sequence.

Q. What advice would you give others who are trying to implement a Team Chart?

The best advice is that you need to really clarify what it is you are trying to accomplish and work back from that. Do your homework on whatever it is you're doing. Look at best practices. Don't try to rubber stamp a form that other people use. It has to be based on your own functions. We have a culture of a minimum of five hours of learning a week for all the staff. And the owner is always reading books and publications, researching, and looking at best practices. It's a constant evolution, as nothing stays the same.

CASE STUDY #2 : Michael Estey, CEO Brand Network, approximately 100 employees

Q. How important is the Team Chart to your organization?

It's vital. Without it, we couldn't really operate. I'd have no idea how the flow lines of the organization were working and what each person was doing. I think we'd be kind of scrambling around in circles if we didn't have that.

We have two organizations, so we have two org charts. I run Brand Network, and my father runs Private Label Beauty & Wellness. I think there are 67 people working at Private Label and 28 at Brand Networks.

It's really the same company, with two different branches. Having an org chart is really important. Even before we hire, the job is laid out on the org chart. We never even interview anybody unless all the responsibilities are clearly delegated in the job posting. Second, we ensure that all the training materials are available for them for that position. We'll have videos and a study roadmap available to them to train and apprentice in that position.

CASE STUDY #3: John Nesbit, CEO Customer Factory, approximately 30 employees

Q. Tell us about your Team Chart.

Our Team Chart is one of the most updated things we have. Being on the Team Chart is how an employee gets plugged into the system. In order to function in our company, you've got to have key results and access to the policies and know who your juniors and seniors are. You get connected. They're not really employed until they're actually on the Team Chart.

We know when someone is definitely no longer employed with us as they are off the Team Chart. It's actually part of our onboarding and offboarding process. You can't really be onboarded with us unless you're in there, because you can't access any of the training–you can't access anything.

Q. What was your business like before having a Team Chart?

There's an inherent loneliness to being an entrepreneur. You're driven by your dream; you have an idea of what you want to create, but it's just you. And even when you bring other people on to help and do various roles in the company, you're still just you, as a team of one trying to get other people to do the things you want to do.

Before I had any kind of concept of a Team Chart, it was just me, and then it was me trying to herd the other people around me to get them to do things and to understand their role. When I put together a Team Chart, I realized that even I wasn't sure what their role was, quite honestly. So if it wasn't clear for me then it definitely wasn't clear for them.

Getting a Team Chart in place forced me, as the business owner, to define the roles. And once I defined the role, I was able to get someone else to do it.

Once they're in that role and they understand it, suddenly, they're a member of the Team. Before that, they're really just an outsider, even if they're sitting right next to you.

It turns a person into a Team member, right then and there, because now they are aligned.

As our company grows, things shift around and change and the flow lines are different. We can embody that in the Team Chart–we just know where it's going to be. So, we change the definition, change the key result, and change a role or a responsibility, and it becomes real immediately because it's changeable. More than half of my staff are now outside the company where they work remotely. So, I have my executives in one place, and the remote staff in another one. There's no way to keep that straight without having the roles and things assigned in a place that everybody can see.

Q. What difference did having a Team Chart make?

Having a Team Chart took me from being one guy in a basement to having 20-plus staff with hundreds of clients. It's a foundational base that you can easily take for granted, thinking it's just some fancy administrative exercise or a waste of time. You might think, "I should work on something more important, like a sales pitch or something," but it's the foundational piece. We wouldn't have the foundation we have without that. We wouldn't have the ability to organize or grow.

We're probably in the top 10% of our industry. Typically, this particular type of business I'm in usually grows to be about one guy and five staff, because that's all one guy can manage. I'm one guy with almost two dozen staff now, and I don't have to manage it all because we have this Team Chart.

There are people out there I call "hustle monsters." They've got to hustle and work 80 hours a week. I don't do that. I leave the office on time to go hang out with my three kids, three cats, and a dog. I don't hustle because things are organized. I don't live in Stressland. I see guys just sweating it, and I've got a business twice that size and it doesn't even hurt. We have our challenges, but I get to leave it here. It doesn't have to bring me in on the weekends; it doesn't grab me by the face and pull me in. It's a game more than a deadly serious activity. So having a Team Chart actually lets you get above the work and be the Game Master. And it's fun. Even when it's going bad, it's still kind of fun. When it's going good, it's really fun. But it shouldn't be stressful. The stress comes from when things aren't being done right below you, and they kind of jump up at you. The Team Chart and the ability to organize lets you push it down to those who are meant to handle those problems.

We have a rule in our company: *No one stays late.* It's a policy actually because I don't want martyrs in my business. I don't want husbands, wives, brothers and sisters, and family members here when they should be with family. I don't want them to be here on the weekend. Nobody comes in on the weekends. That's against what we stand for. When you're properly organized and things work, you should be able to get all your work done easily during the day. Otherwise, there's something wrong. Your employees shouldn't feel like they have to stay all night or come in early or die at their desk. Who wants to work in a place like that? There's no price you can put on simplifying your life or making things so that your business doesn't destroy your life. You can have a nice business without it eating up your entire life. I know that by not having a Team Chart and having a stressful business, you're paying a very high price.

Q. How long did it take you to implement your Team Chart?

It took about three or four days to set up what I had in mind. It forced me to really look at all the departments that exist in the business. Where does the legal compliance go in my world? Who takes care of the toilet paper in the office? Those had to be somewhere on the chart. Those responsibilities have to go on there somewhere. Where do our new leads come in, and where do they get sold? It really forced me to think all the way through it. So that was probably a good three or four days, but I'll be honest, I feel like it's actually never quite done because there's always improvements to be made. When we have a new initiative, where does that go? Who's going to do that? We have to organize that so it doesn't become a problem. It's not something you set and forget.

Q. What advice would you give to others who haven't implemented a Team Chart?

If you don't have a Team Chart, you're missing the boat. And if you're too busy or overwhelmed to do it, then that's more reason why you must create one. The reason you're so dang busy and overwhelmed is because you don't have a Team Chart.

Just bite the bullet, take a long weekend, and start.

And here's a piece of advice: *Perfect* is the enemy of *good* when it comes to your Team Chart. You're going to want to make a perfect chart, but it won't be perfect. It'll be good. Go for good, and make good a little better as you go along. Half organized is better than not organized at all. Then go for 60% organized and 70% organized. Eventually, you will get up to 99% organized. You'll never get that last percentage because business changes and things happen.

CASE STUDY #4: Manuel Suárez, Founder & CEO of Attention Grabbing Media (AGM), 80 employees and President of Natural Slim, 150 employees. Author of Marketing Magic.

Q. Tell us about your Team Chart.

I have two companies, and revising the Team Chart is a never-ending process. It gets adjusted, improved, corrected, and optimized to try to build a better team. The challenge is, how do you get the most value out of a particular person? Having a Team Chart makes that person become more valuable to the organization.

Natural Slim is a big company. It's going to do $80 million this year. It has a chain of command with departments, department heads, and so on. But at AGM, the marketing company, we had to consistently tweak the Team Chart. The latest version seemed to be the perfect one. Turns out, it wasn't.

Q. What challenges did you face implementing your Team Chart?

You've got to be willing to adjust, which happens whenever you release a new version, but it puts more order in place. I think one of the most important things about having a Team Chart is that duties and responsibilities are clearly established; it also helps having seniors and juniors in place. That, for me, is crucial, and the Team Chart allows us to have that in place. You can't simply clock in and click out; there's a person to communicate with above you. There's only one person in this company who doesn't have somebody above them, and that's me. Everybody else has to have somebody to report to. Some have people under them they also have to be responsible for. When they're not responsible for them, the organization falls apart–the people are operating on their own, so productivity collapses.

Not having a Team Chart is not a reason to not succeed, but it definitely slows you down. It stops the scalability of your company and how much you can accomplish. I have succeeded by sheer determination to succeed, but this machine would have grown more if I would have started earlier on the creation of a Team Chart.

Q. What results have you noticed since implementing a Team Chart?

I feel that I'm just getting started in this organizational process because I have a big vision for this company and its potential. I have a company that has accomplished a lot of great things; reputation-wise, we are an industry-leading marketing agency. Within the first three years of operation, we made the Inc. 5000 List. But I think we would have achieved more if we had had a proper Team Chart because I know we lost talent early on.

We lost people who could have been valuable. Because I didn't have a Team Chart, they didn't know how to provide value. We expected them to flourish on their own.

When our Team Chart was properly established, we were able to recruit people better, and they were able to get in there and know exactly what was needed. They knew who they needed to report to, who their juniors and seniors were, what value was expected from them, and if they were providing value or not.

The great majority of the people in the world are employees. Entrepreneurs are the ones who take risks, and they are rare. Most people need stability, and the Team Chart provides stability. You cannot really expand without a Team Chart.

Q. What advice would you give others who are trying to implement a Team Chart?

In my opinion, the most important division of the entire organization is recruitment. If your company is hiring low-quality personnel, then you're going to have a low-quality service company. Your recruiters need the ability to detect talent, to bring in qualified people, and to create processes and key results. One of the most costly things is paying people who don't know what value they are giving to the organization. When you hire somebody, if you don't give them a job, if you don't give them a responsibility, and if you don't define exact results, you're going to end up wasting money that you could have used to grow the company. There are two main reasons why a company might fall apart. One of them is the recruitment area, and the other one is marketing. If you don't do marketing, you don't get attention. If you can't get attention; you cannot sell anything. But in terms of recruitment, if you don't get the right people, you're going to fall apart too.

CASE STUDY #5: Selwyn Duijvestijn, CEO, DGB Group, approximately 101 employees

Q. Tell us about your Team Chart.

We were always looking for a structure but never followed a methodology or a very clear organizational overview. Now we have a Team Chart, and it has really helped structure everything. It remains a key project to maintain as it gives insights to everyone, because it's not a piece of paper you keep in your drawer. It's like a tool you use.

Q. What was the result after implementing your Team Chart?

I would say that the first result was that there was a lot of clarity. People know exactly what they're doing, and they are very clear about what they need to do. The result is there's more organization and therefore there's growth.

Q. How long did it take to implement?

I would say that making sure it fit our business model was the first step. Step number 2 would be to get the first ten people to embrace it and love it. Everyone is now on board. It makes a lot of sense, because they step into a structure, and then it goes quite easily.

It took about half a year of being very strict and saying, "That's not your post. That's not your job. As per the Team Chart, you should be doing this, not that."

Now, it's just clear to everyone.

Q. Did you as the founder and CEO have to be the one to push it, to develop the culture?

Yeah, definitely. It was also my wife, who is also very involved in the business, and then later we had a Chief of Staff, a very organized editor as well. He says, "I don't care what the system is as long as there's a system," which is a very good way to operate. That really kick-started it—when key people in the organization decided we needed a system.

Q. What advice would you give to others who are trying to implement a Team Chart?

I would say take the time and energy and attention to making a clear structure for yourself in the beginning, because when you start, like every entrepreneur, you have many different roles. I think 99% of people want to grow and expand, but then you need to dive in deeper and ask yourself how you are going to do that. Making revenue go up is great, but then what? How are you going to actually manage that growth? So my advice would be to think of your Team Chart in the beginning because you will eventually need it when you expand. We're managing 5 big projects, but it's doable with our current structure, but we want to grow to 500, and that's how we're building our business. All we need to do is build 10 more structures of what we currently have. So our goal is to get it right so all we have to do is duplicate it.

Building Block 3:

Every Player Has One or More Key Results

Imagine a sport where nobody kept score. It wouldn't be much of a game. Take away that one element and the game disappears, as does the fun, triumph, motivation, and joy.

Business is the same.

All sports have a key measure of performance that determines whether you win or lose. It might be scoring goals, runs, bases, or beating the clock—no matter what it is, it is measured. Let's call this, simply, the goal.

In addition to the goal, there are other results that are also measured, such as assists in scoring, defending actions of blocking an opposing team, number of passes, speed of changing tires, lap times, and so on.

In any sport, the achievement of winning is a combination of the little results, each one adding to the next, with the result of winning the game, the tournament, the world title.

In sports, all of it is measured. Each player knows how their actions contributed to the overall win. They even have awards for outstanding achievers. Players are recognised for their results, and because they are measured, each player knows going into every new game exactly what they need to do to beat their prior performance, to be better, to contribute more to the Team.

Although business is a game, unfortunately, the same attention is not given to _all_ the players. Often, in business, only those directly involved in the "Big Goal" get acknowledged. The ones who get a pat on the back, a bonus, a trophy are the "Top Sales Person" or the CEO who "generated" more profits.

But what about the person in accounting, working diligently, ensuring income and expenses are tracked and reported on time? How would the CEO even know if they were growing a profitable business without such a star player in the accounts department?

Consider also the Recruitment Manager who hired the star salesperson and the CEO, the technical team who kept all of the computers working, the Sales Trainer who coached the star salesperson, the delivery team who made sure the client got what was promised and turned them into a referral machine giving the star salesperson new prospects, and let's not forget the janitor who ensured that all the clients and players arrived at beautifully maintained premises every day.

Every single person on the Team is a player. And *every player has one or more key results.* If you don't measure it, you don't have a True Team. A game can only exist if you keep score; without a score, there is no game. A player without a measured key result has no game, and work becomes a chore.

On the flipside, a player who knows their key results is motivated, focused, and aligned. They become Totally Engaged Aligned Members.

So far, we've covered these 3 Foundational Building Blocks:

1. There Has to Be a Reason to Play
2. Every Player Has a Position on the Team Chart
3. Every Player Has One or More Key Results

Understanding and implementing just these Building Blocks will change your business forever.

If you take a look at the True Team Blueprint below, you'll see these 3 Foundational Building Blocks are the base of a True Team. Everything else we'll cover builds on these three building blocks and makes them stronger. Take these three away and you lose the game, you lose the Team, and everything comes crashing down.

Never forget the importance of a reason to play, the position of every player on your Team Chart, and the measurement of their key results.

Finding the Key Results

For most players on your Team Chart, defining the key results is simple. However, there are some roles where it might be difficult. For example, how do you measure the performance of a receptionist or janitor? Before we answer that, it's worth knowing that key results can be measured in the following ways:

1. Amount (number of something)
2. Value (monetary or assigned value)
3. Percentage (e.g., % jobs delivered on time, % of collected accounts, % of fully trained staff)

4. Feedback (a positive or negative rating system. But be sure to avoid the use of feelings, opinions, and subjective measures for the basis of a key result, as these inevitably become inaccurate and irrelevant.)

Let's take a look at the role of a janitor who gets paid to clean the entire office. We expect the place to be vacuumed and dusted, trash removed, and disposables restocked. Trying to individually track all these functions is cumbersome. Well, how do you know if the cleaning was done? That's obvious, as you'd see dirt, dust, and trash piling up and the restrooms running out of toilet paper. So the best way to track the production of a janitor is to count what has NOT been done. This can be achieved using the feedback method, and the easiest way to do that is to provide the entire Team with a way to submit a janitor report. The janitor's key result is the number of reports submitted or the number of areas affected, and the goal of the janitor is zero! (Note: the graph below is what we call an inverted graph, with zero at the top. That way, by looking at the graph, you know up = good)

Janitor Report & Key Results Graph

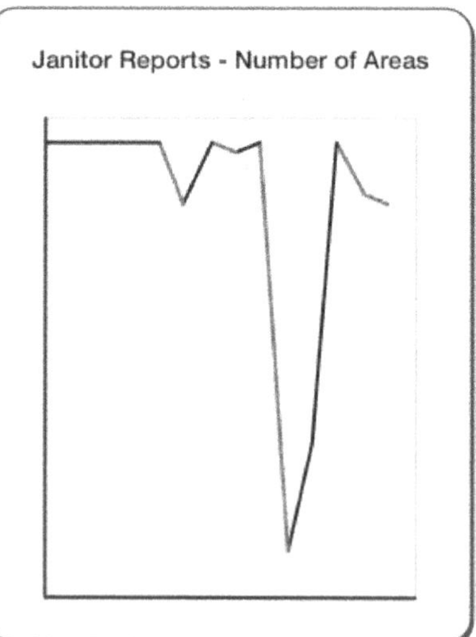

Tracking the productivity of a receptionist depends on the main functions of the role. If their main task is to answer phones, then you could simply track the number of answered calls and perhaps the length of time callers spend on hold. This is easy to do in today's electronic world. If the receptionist meets and greets clients, then you could count the number of meetings the receptionist helps facilitate. Another important function of a receptionist is to ensure all communications are passed onto the correct person in a timely manner. A receptionist who is constantly routing calls to the wrong department is not a Team player; therefore, as with the janitor, an alert system (feedback method) could also be used by the Team, who report on incorrectly routed calls.

The thing to remember is that every player has a measurable key result that aligns with the reason they are playing in that position on the Team. They are there to do a job, and they are paid to get a specific result. The result is *always* measurable. Sometimes it takes a little trial and error to get the right key result. If you get stuck or want some ideas, we can put you in contact with one of our MetaPulse Specialists, just reach out to our support team at metapulse.com for help.

Case Studies

We asked several clients who successfully implemented this Building Block about the challenges they faced and the difference it made to their business. Here's what they had to say.

CASE STUDY #1: Company Name Withheld, approximately 1,800 employees

Q. Tell us how you use key results.

Every single person has a key result, a minimum of one, but they have a particular named key result they have to achieve each quarter.

Q. What challenges did you face implementing key results?

It took us a couple of quarters to really get in the groove on it. We did a couple of iterations. The biggest barrier was getting everyone on the same page about how to do it. Some people weren't familiar with tracking or monitoring what they did.

Some would monitor sales, but what are all the actions it takes to get there? And it's different for different types of sales teams or other parts of the company that support that, so you have to really understand your organization and how everyone works together. In order to make it a successful system, you have to identify the measurements that are going to be the most useful. And you might want to measure some additional things for yourself, but in the big picture, they weren't necessarily critical for everyone to pay attention to.

Q. What advice would you give others who are trying to implement key results?

It's critical, so do it. Work it out, spend the time, do the homework. Monitor everything you possibly can and identify relationships between the things you are monitoring. It also becomes formulaic. You push for X, Y, Z key results, and by achieving those results, you experience an improvement elsewhere, so it all works together.

CASE STUDY #2 : Michael Estey, CEO Brand Network, approximately 100 employees

Q. How important are key results?

They're everything. You see how effective your Team is immediately. The staff's collective key results are a reflection of how productive the entire Team is. You really see the weak points very quickly. If you see something not getting done, or it seems like there's just holes of some kind, it's very easy to review the key results to find out where they're coming from–which department, which section, which division, or which executive. Having those measurements there, which are attributable to a position or to an individual on the Team Chart, means you can find the weak points and correct them fast. Otherwise, you're literally running the organization completely blind. Maybe you're on a streak of luck and can get by without them, but that's luck. It's going to run out sooner or later. For instance, last year, there was a giant event that resulted in 10x income for about one quarter; one of our brands went viral on TikTok. So, we marked that event; that way, whenever we're reviewing the key results and saying, "Oh look how well we were doing," we know why.

For instance, Christmas week is very slow in E-commerce. People buy two weeks leading up to Christmas, but they don't buy the week of Christmas. We know that because we see it. It's very easy to find the ups and downs and plan accordingly.

CASE STUDY #3: John Nesbit, CEO Customer Factory, approximately 30 employees

Q. Tell us how you use key results.

We have 100 graphs or more, but it didn't start that way. We started with five. Now for every post in my company, every person has at least one that they measure. This is the great equalizer in the company, because it gets rid of office politics. When someone has something they're measured by, and it's an objective measurement, there's no guessing if the guy is productive or not.

Everybody knows where they stand.

We grew by 30% because we have the ability to see what makes a difference in the business. Everybody looks at gross income, how much money we make, or how many clients we have, and they can be proud of that. Let's say it goes down a little bit or even goes up a little bit. You might ask why. How can you stop it from going down more? You can't solve that mystery very easily unless you have all the other key results and subgraphs. Somewhere in there, you'll find another graph that went down. You can look down there and find it and the subgraph that went down too. And there's another one. Oh, those two made that one go down. Okay, so we know what to fix. I can't just yell and make more income. I have to figure out what went down. The same applies when you see things go up dramatically. I look and find out the things that pushed it, and then I enshrine those as policy for the company forever and ever. We do more of this stuff that made it go up, and we avoid repeating the thing that made it go down.

People think running a business is hard. It's actually not that hard. You just do more of the good and less of the bad, but you've got to be able to see what's going on. That's what key results are for. If you don't have those, you don't know.

We actually had a recent down period, and I was able to see right when it started. I was able to see all the things that contributed to it and immediately start to revert it. When I see why, I'm able to relax about it because I know how to fix it. It's just a matter of executing. As an entrepreneur, that's what we do–we execute.

Q. How long did it take you to implement key results?

It took literally five minutes to say, "Let's track income. Let's track clients." It's easy to start naming off key results, and then it just got more and more sophisticated over time. It became a policy that everybody in the company has their own graphs, and all the graphs have to add up to something worthwhile.

It takes minutes a week to keep the system up to date. It's super easy.

Q. What advice would you give others who are trying to implement key results?

If you want to build your business blind and in the dark, go ahead and don't measure key results. If you want to know what's going on and know who's actually productive and who's not for real, and if you want to make good decisions based on actual data and not fantasies, then you've got to have key results. You've got to have these numbers in front of you. Why suffer? It's not like this is hard to do.

I would say if you want to avoid bombs and blow-ups, get your key results figured out–you'll be surprised.

Entrepreneurs are usually optimistic by nature. There's a self-delusion that's sometimes part of the game, and you might think you're doing better than you actually are. Or you might not see something that's actually rotten in your organization. For example, it's very easy to have increasing income and bad delivery. You think the income is going to go on forever, and then it just collapses because you didn't catch that delivery was going badly. That's what key results are for; it keeps things real.

CASE STUDY #4: Manuel Suárez, Founder & CEO of Attention Grabbing Media (AGM), 80 employees and President of Natural Slim, 150 employees. Author of *Marketing Magic*.

Q. Tell us how you use key results.

This is very important. Cash is oxygen for a business, and if you don't have enough oxygen, you're going to die. I get a report every morning that includes collections, money still to be collected, new money coming in, sales, etc. I get a report on all of it. Since I'm the best salesman in this company, if we're not on track each month, I jump all over that. I had one month where I lost money: March 2020. We all know what was going on at that time! That's the only month in my entire life that I've lost money. It was a scary and concerning time. We got back on track. I implemented a strategy in that particular month to get more attention. We got more business, and we never had to let anyone go.

I believe attention is the driver of oxygen; it is essential to your organization. Obviously, I'm obsessed with marketing. I'm always trying to figure out how to get more attention.

I get reports of progress. Some executives want to keep things off their plate, but I want things on my plate. In my company, if you keep things off my plate, you're going to get in a lot of trouble. If you are in my company, then you communicate with me. Every single morning, when my employees check in at 8:30am, they spend the first 5-10 minutes writing down their plan, what they want to accomplish for that day, and what key results they're going to achieve. This is our policy, and if you break these policies, you're out.

Each person needs to send their report to their senior, and their senior must acknowledge it. At the end of the day, they have to do an end-of-day report. On Friday mornings, each person does a weekly report that explains what was accomplished that week and what they're looking to accomplish in the next week. That creates a Team with accountability across the organization.

Q. What challenges did you face implementing key results?

Everybody has one key result. But I'll be honest, some things took a lot of figuring out because we do so many different services. We deliver Amazon services, we do Facebook and Instagram ads, and we build personal brands. We do email marketing and text messages. One of the challenges that we ran into was with video editors–how could we measure their production?

We have 50 editors on staff, and some of the videos that they do are one minute long; other videos are 20 minutes long, so you can't measure just one piece of content. Currently we have a key result for every area, and each person knows how to measure themselves and their productivity. But it took a lot to get to this point, especially with so many different and moving parts. It's more difficult for a service-based business, but it is vital.

Q. What difference did it make implementing key results?

There is more predictability. We are more consistent in our ability to produce quality services to our clients, and we have better processes in place to pick up when things need to be corrected.

Now we are able to set expectations for new clients. We tell them, this is what the journey at AGM looks like, this is what the process looks like, and this is what you can expect. We're at the stage right now where everybody understands those concepts at Attention Grabbing Media. We're able to systematically hire people who can produce value, because we know how to put them on the Team Chart. Then we systematically bring in new clients, get them serviced, and get them results. This is tough to do in the agency world. Natural Slim was a piece of cake compared to this, but we worked it out.

CASE STUDY #5: Selwyn Duijvestijn, CEO, DGB Group, approximately 101 employees

Q. Tell us about your key results and how you use them.

Everyone working in the business has to have at least one key result, but ideally two or three key results per role. A sales role is very straightforward; you track revenue incoming. For a graphic designer, it's more difficult, so you need to get quite creative to figure out what to measure. We settled on the amount of visuals created; now, we measure all sorts of things like new contacts asking for information, site visitors, portfolio size, and more. But everyone has at least one to measure.

Q. What was your business like before you started measuring key results?

It was less clear and less certain. We didn't know if we were doing really well or not. Now we can see it, and it becomes very clear why you're happy or not happy. Each person knows, "Oh, I'm going down; this is not good. I'm not doing something correct." This is much better than thinking you're doing really well and then it's a surprise to hear, "Oh, you're actually not."

In Dutch we say *alle neuzen*, which translates to "all noses in the same direction." There's a few of these Dutch sayings that sound weird in English, but it perfectly explains what has become the company culture. We all have the same clear goal. If you look at the key results of a division, it's very clear for everyone in that division. That's what we're going for as a Team.

Q. How long did it take to implement measuring key results for your Team, and what challenges did you face?

Implementing key results for the sales team took a minute; it just got done.

The salespeople love it. They love to see it; they love to go for it. Other roles were more difficult, for example with us, there is a project design function, and we have a Project Design Manager. He will spend 2-3 months working on one document. So we had to think of the structure with the Team Chart and figure out how to measure someone on a week-by-week basis. We're happy if he delivers in 2 months and not in 2 and a half as long as the quality is good. So figuring out his key results actually made us put in a lot more structure and organization. Now he focuses on creating new chapters and getting one completed each week. So, we could actually measure the results on a weekly basis. That took some time, and it's still ongoing actually, but we're making sure that there's more standardization so we get better results. But it is worth it because it's now ready for growth.

Building Block 4:

Key Results Are Shared and Monitored

In the prior Building Block #3, we discussed the importance of assigning one or more key results to every player.

The next phase of this is to share them with your Team so that everyone can know what they are and monitor them.

Simple Key Results

The best way to track key results is to use line graphs, where up is good and down is bad.

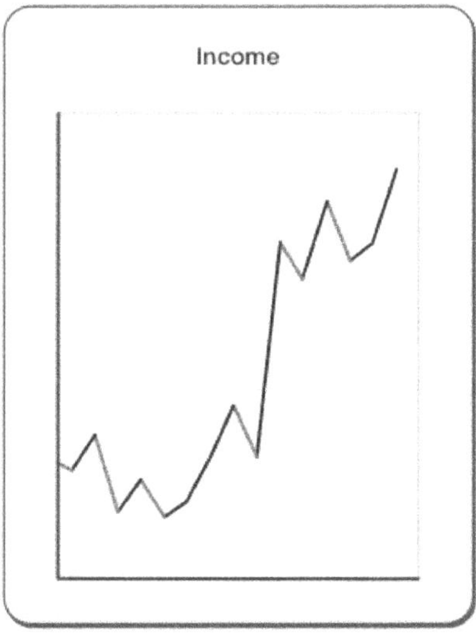

In the case of a "negative result," such as refunds (or the janitor example we shared in the prior chapter), where you want the result to be as close to zero as possible, then the graph values are inverted, with zero at the top. That way, the simple principle still applies—up is good and down is bad, and you don't have to do mental gymnastics when viewing multiple graphs.

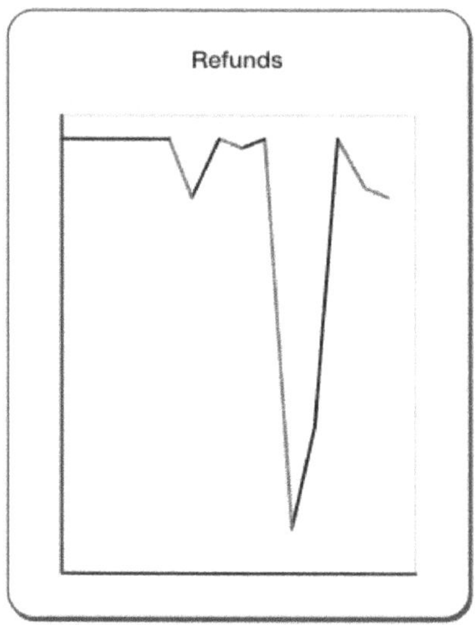

With this simple method, players and managers can easily review their performance and the performance of the entire team and know if things are improving:

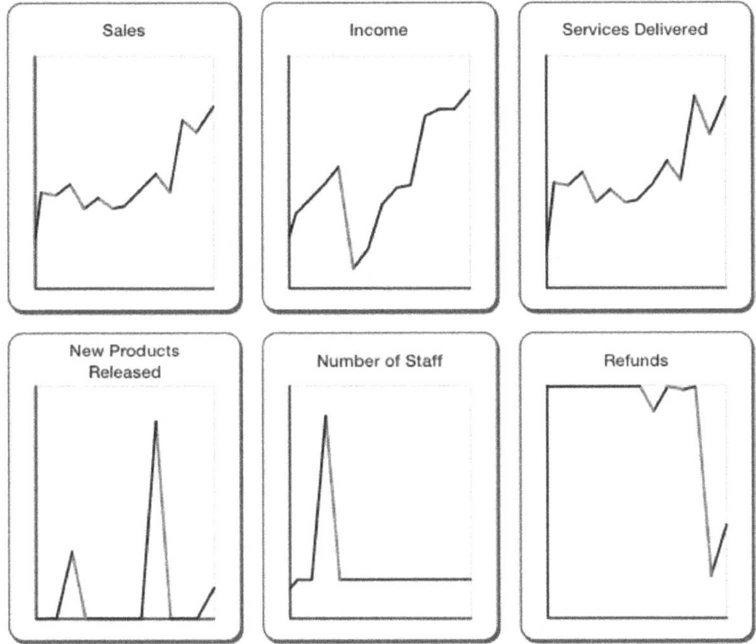

Players should track their results daily with the aim of beating last week's or last month's performance.

Those higher on the Team Chart take a broader view, looking at performance over a monthly or quarterly period. However, a good manager always pays attention to the details and should have the ability to easily see the weekly and daily progress.

Building a Results-Based Culture

Tracking key results for all players is a culture that must be driven from the top down. The Founder or CEO needs to be the one who demands to see key results and who leads by example by tracking their own performance.

From experience, we've found it's best to track key results daily. Make it a habit for every player to enter their key results at the end of the day or the prior day's results first thing every morning. While much of the data entry can be automated in today's online world, getting every player to view and track their results on a graph is necessary. Afterall, if they never *look* at the graph, they may as well not be keeping score. And that, as you now know, destroys a True Team.

Once the Team is imbued with a *Results-based Culture,* you will witness it take on a life of its own. Your Team will become a magnet for star players who are hungry for key results, just as a sports star is hungry to score goals and win.

Simple Decisions

With key results at your fingertips, business decisions become easier. Rather than operating off of a whim or a rumor, all players can confidently assess the current situation using key results. Is Janet a good receptionist? Take a look at her key results; they will give you an idea. Is Fred a good janitor? Again, the key results are a good place to look before you decide. But if you don't have such information easily accessible, then you have to rely on opinions and rumors, and that's a very dangerous method of running a business and creating a Team. In fact, True Teams are destroyed by opinions and rumors.

Start with the Basics

To get started, we suggest getting every Team member to identify at least one key result they want to measure that reflects their performance. No doubt in the future they'll want to measure more key results, or they may even change what they measure, and that's okay. The important step is that every player starts to measure and monitor at least one key result. Make it a daily habit and watch your Team come to life.

Case Studies

We asked several clients who had successfully implemented this Building Block about the challenges they faced and what difference it made to their business. Here's what they had to say:

CASE STUDY #1: Company Name Withheld, approximately 1,800 employees

Q. Tell us how you share your key results

In our company, we have a policy of radical transparency so everything is visible to every single staff 24/7. We have the major ones posted in obvious places. To prevent siloing, we encourage people to look at some additional key results in areas outside of their own. Sharing key results has helped us achieve hyper growth.

Q. What about sharing financial information?

The more information a person has, the better able he is able to do something with it. We go through extra steps in our hiring process to hire people that we trust, and we treat them like adults. We don't have any reason for anything to be hidden.

CASE STUDY #2: John Nesbit, CEO Customer Factory, approximately 30 employees

Q. Tell us how you share your key results.

I feel strongly about this. Every graph is available on the wall printed every week for all staff to see. And for the remote staff, they all have access to every graph, company reserves, income, everything, because I want them to know where they stand. When things are good, they know why I'm in a good mood. And when things are down, they know why I'm being a little more strict. They know why I'm pushing a little harder on something. There are no mysteries because if you don't tell people facts, they will invent something else. They'll think, "Well, they're not telling us how much money they're making because they're making millions, and they're just screwing us over," something silly like that.

I'm very transparent. I find it makes for a more responsible Team because they know what's going on. They're in control of their own jobs, and they know how their job contributes to the rest of the organization. When that graph goes up, it's everybody's collective group activity. We actually use that to play games, like when the company hits a certain level, we're going to do a bonus. We actually have one where when we hit a certain level, we have raises across the board. Another one is when we hit this level, everybody gets a week's pay as a bonus. So, they can't wait to see that graph, and when the graph goes down, they're not happy. It's not my graph anymore. It's their graph.

When you try to manage people top down and force them to do things and try to get them to do stuff that you cannot really achieve, that's hard to do. Even being forceful or angry doesn't work; you've got to get the group to do it to themselves. So once everybody in the group realizes their own personal future and prosperity is determined by how well these key results are doing, they'll encourage each other; they'll help each other to make the number even though it's not even their job. They'll catch the bomb before it goes off. It gets everybody pulling the same rope. You're not walking around as the only one to tell people what to do. I think that gives people a certain respect and a certain comfort with their job, because they know where they're at. And they know if the numbers are down, they know the problem and they know they've got to fix it.

Q. What was it like before you started sharing all this information?

It was lonely. You're doing stuff, and you're having a bad day because the numbers are down, but everyone else is bopping around, like nothing's happening, and you're like, "Don't you guys realize we have a burn rate all of a sudden?"

Now there's much more team coordination. Most people will do a good job if you give them the time, space, and information to do that job. The key piece of information is to show them how things are going, and you do that with key results.

Q. What about sharing financial information?

Oh, of course, there's that first question, "Should we share the financial data?" You know, that's supposed to be a secret, right?"

Well, we actually have a measurement that I think is useful. We take the number of staff and the amount of income, and we divide it by the number of staff as one of our key results, and that number goes up and up and up and up. That's because we measure it, and it's managed, and everyone knows where they are. So, everyone wants to get their key results going up. Every week, we go over every department, and they share their numbers. Here it is, and here's how it's going. Everybody can see it, so there's no hiding here. And also, I'll tell you this, when you are hiring, and you tell the person that you are going to be measuring their production, they're two responses you get: "Oh, no," and, "Oh, good." You hire the "Oh, goods." and you pass over the "Oh, nos." It keeps away the ones who are just looking for a place to park and put their hours in. It gets you the True Team members who actually want to play the game with you. You really can't beat that feeling when you see everybody pulling on the same rope, and we're all trying to survive better as a group than as a bunch of individuals.

I can't think of any other way to manage things. I don't know how people do it without it, really.

CASE STUDY #3: Manuel Suárez, Founder & CEO of Attention Grabbing Media (AGM), 80 employees and President of Natural Slim, 150 employees. Author of *Marketing Magic.*

Q. How do you share your key results?

Every morning, we have a 15-minute Team meeting. All division heads share what's happening in their area. For example, the head of delivery will talk about the results clients are getting. So, the entire organization knows who we're working for. All results are open and transparent, including sales and revenue. We give people an update on our targets and our goals. We want to get them on the same page with us and what we're trying to accomplish. As a leader, this is important because a lot of leaders, entrepreneurs, CEOs, etc. don't want employees to know the revenue numbers, probably because they're not giving enough to their team.

When this happens, employees start thinking, "I'm doing all this work to make my boss rich." That's a sign of a broken culture. I give my staff so much. I give them retirement plans and paid vacation time, which I don't have to do in the state of Florida. I give them great salaries, which are above the average household. I give them great opportunities, evaluations, parties, and a fun and safe working environment. When the company wins, everybody wins. Nobody is left behind.

CASE STUDY #4: Selwyn Duijvestijn, CEO, DGB Group, approximately 101 employees

Q. Tell us how you share your key results.

We're a public company, so everything is already public. We integrate MetaPulse with Slack so everyone can easily see how each division is doing. It's in your face. But anyone can go to the Team Chart and see everyone's results and see what's going well and what's not.

Q. What about sharing financial information—do you share that with your Team?

I definitely do. That's becoming more and more of a main driver for what I'm doing every day.

Q. Did you notice a difference in the Team when you started sharing everything and showing them all key results, compared to before?

It became easier to implement things. By sharing, we're not forcing that on only you. No, we're doing it throughout the entire organization, and by sharing it's like, "Oh, they're also doing it there and they're also doing it there, and it's happening in all different divisions." You can see who is doing well. It makes it easier.

Q. Did you notice any difference in terms of business growth?

Well, the best example would be in the content Team because that was harder to do initially. We do projects throughout Africa. We have a cinematographer taking pictures, making videos, and someone managing social media. There's an editor, there's a copywriter, there's a graphic designer, and there's a marketeer. We explained to them, "These are your results; you are focussing on getting new people in, and also on getting leads, and then together with the sales, they convert it into a sale." It really created a team effort, and we put a financial bonus to it as well, to really incentivize it and to keep them focused on the key results. From that moment on, the results went up and up, and they keep going up.

Q. Did you face any challenges when you began sharing all key results?

Definitely. When we started implementing this, there was some resistance from people who said, "I cannot be measured. I'm just doing the best I can. I'm always doing well. Why are you concerned about my results?"

We replied with, "Then why is there a problem measuring it?" Now everyone involved loves it, because they're proud of what they do, and they say, "I want my results to be measured, because I'm doing great and I can even do better." But in the beginning, there were some who resisted, and those are the exact same people who are no longer working with us. Not because we fired them; they just left, and it didn't work out for them.

Q. What advice would you give to others about sharing key results, especially financial ones?

I can see some people might not want to share financial results, but we are a public company so everything is public anyways. But I think if you have the right people, they should know and they will go for it, and it will really hold the Team together because if you do well as a Team, then everyone does better.

Players Need Knowledge to Know How to Play

It has been said that knowledge is power, and it's true. It's also said that ignorance is bliss; however, this statement is not true. In fact, ignorance is dangerous. Imagine letting someone drive a Formula One car without any training or knowledge. If you just handed them the keys and wished them well, disaster would unfold.

Yet in business, we expect people to do a job well with little orientation or knowledge. People get hired or given roles, and they are expected to do a good job without being shown the rules of the game and how to keep score. In contrast, sporting professionals spend years training and learning.

To combat "player ignorance," new hires are expected to have "experience." It is assumed that experience = knowledge and skill, but that is not always the case. The true test of a person's knowledge is whether they can get results, so a person's results are far more important than the knowledge and experience they have.

A far better way to build a True Team is to provide them with the knowledge they need to win.

To do that requires the following:

1. Knowing what gets results.
2. Recording that knowledge.
3. Sharing that knowledge with every Team member.
4. Ensuring that knowledge is being studied.

5. Ensuring that knowledge is being applied.
6. Reissuing needed knowledge if key results falter.

Knowing What Gets Results

Most businesses, as they grow, figure out what works and what doesn't. This is a natural process. To survive and thrive, a True Team must learn how to get results.

Unfortunately that hard-won knowledge is seldom recorded or documented. Often, it "sits in the head" of those who learned it the hard way. It gets passed to others and new recruits in a careless and unplanned way, or it may not be passed on at all, unless a mistake is made and one is reminded of the "right way" to do it.

Knowing how to get results is priceless knowledge. It should be treated as you would a precious gemstone. Once learned, it should be recorded in some way, either written, spoken, or filmed. And that is very easy to do today.

Here's a simple example: We know of an owner of a property inspection business. When it came time to train others exactly how to do an inspection, he simply attached a camera to a hard hat he wore and recorded half a dozen inspections, verbally describing each step he took. That video was broken up into sections and became the "Property Inspectors Course." It had everything a new recruit needed to know to perform a property inspection and to *get the same result* as the owner. With this knowledge recorded, it was easy to share. By creating a course, he ensured the knowledge was studied. The final step of ensuring the knowledge was applied was simply a matter of accompanying the newly trained recruits on several inspections and reviewing their inspection reports. If the new recruit failed to follow standard procedure during the inspection, they were instructed to re-study that part of the course. With this method, the owner was able to grow his business to twenty-six franchisees in less than two years, and none of the inspectors had prior experience. They didn't need it. They were given the knowledge they needed to win.

Sharing Knowledge

Of all the Building Blocks, this is perhaps the toughest to implement, yet it is vital to building a rapidly expanding profitable business. If you have ever tried to create standard procedures or policy in a business, you know the key challenges are figuring out the following details:

1. Where is the policy/procedure stored, and what is it called?
2. Who needs to study it?
3. Have they studied it?
4. Which version was studied?
5. When did they study it?
6. Who needs to re-study this update?
7. Have they studied the update?
8. When did they study the update?

It's a mammoth task to create, maintain, and distribute knowledge. It's also a mammoth task tracking and enforcing the study progress of every Team member. It's no wonder why so few businesses keep knowledge and why so many businesses struggle. But there are only four simple habits you need to develop to master this vital Building Block.

Successful Habits

1. **Record your knowledge** - Avoid training your Team with verbal instructions that are not recorded, as the information is easily forgotten or lost. Write it down in a way that can be easily shared or record an audio or video of your know-how.
2. **Share the knowledge medium** - Don't repeat yourself. Share the written or recorded medium. Always direct your Team to the written or recorded knowledge. If it's not written or recorded, then do number 1 above.
3. **Organize the knowledge** - Ensure the knowledge is stored and named so it can easily be found by anyone on the Team.

4. **Create a culture of "knowledge first"** - The solution to any problem you encounter in business should be met with the "knowledge-first" approach, as illustrated in the following flowchart.

Knowledge-first Culture Approach

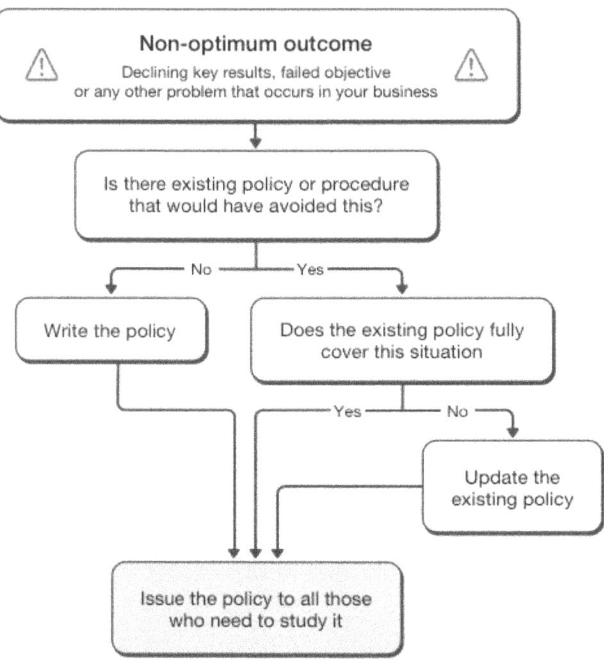

Identifying Knowledge Gaps

Once you understand the power of the knowledge system, *any* problem in business is answered simply by saying, "Read the policy; here's the link," or, "Let's write a policy so everyone knows how to handle this situation in the future."

To drive the point home, note that in the prior sentence, we mentioned "*any* problem in business." This truly is a magic bullet to all business difficulties, but rather than look upon them as problems, we prefer to call them knowledge gaps, because that's what they really are.

As a business owner your first priority is to close the knowledge gaps. These occur as you grow. The knowledge gaps show up in declining key results, failed objectives, complaints voiced by players, or you as the owner being overworked. All such things have the same solution: close the knowledge gap. Just follow the flowchart process provided above and get the knowledge known.

Then the game of business becomes so much easier to win.

Your First Knowledge Items

Where do you start? What knowledge does your Team need to know?

You can begin by sharing the principles of the Foundational Building Blocks discussed in this book; that's Building Blocks 1, 2, and 3.

Simply write something about your reason for playing the game, why the business is here, what your overall goals are, and why you built the business.

Create some knowledge about the Team Chart and why it's needed.

Tell your Team that they are expected to track key results and to work out what they are for each Team member.

Another way to share knowledge is to share existing knowledge. We know a very successful entrepreneur who gets his entire Team to read about half a dozen business books when they join his Team. This ensures everyone is operating within the same culture. They understand the key terms and phrases everyone uses. You could even start with this book. That's a very simple way to get your entire Team working together and implementing the True Team Building Blocks.

Thankfully, MetaPulse makes the storing and sharing of knowledge very easy. The main benefits are due to the Team-centric nature of the app. The Team Chart is used to determine who needs to study what. This simplifies the distribution process. Furthermore, MetaPulse tracks each version of the policy and, as part of the distribution process, it's possible to have Team members acknowledge that they have studied the policy, that they understand it, and that they will apply it. But you don't need to use MetaPulse to implement this Building Block. Google Docs or other similar document systems are a good start. Although they don't have the Team Chart-centric distribution feature, they still allow you to create and share policy.

Case Studies

We asked several clients who had successfully implemented this Building Block about the challenges they faced and what difference it made to their business. Here's what they had to say:

CASE STUDY #1: Company Name Withheld, approximately 1,800 employees

Q. Tell us how you use knowledge.

We love this. This is really fabulous because we had our policies and knowledge articles in discrete locations, and sometimes you couldn't remember where it was or how to find it. Now we utilize the knowledge section within Metapulse to have all our policies in one place, and it's awesome!

Q. What challenges did you face implementing knowledge?

We started documenting things from the beginning, but challenges were on giving people things that were relevant to their position, or just making things accessible that were relevant, as you couldn't always anticipate who needed something because they might be in an unassociated area, not directly in an area, but they had something they were doing that was very similar. They could either follow that procedure or adapt it for their own use. We ran into so much confusion earlier on not knowing where to go for that.

It was confusing. You'd know there was a reference [policy or procedure] that could help, but you'd end up getting delayed or sometimes you couldn't get access to it, so you did something incorrectly and caused a lot of extra work by not having it. Now everyone knows where to go to get it.

Q. What benefits has sharing knowledge brought to your business?

It's really easy to refer someone to a reference [policy or procedure]. If they are new and they are asking questions, it's easy to show that person exactly where to go, and people are able to look things up. You can refresh your own knowledge on an area; you just go search and you can find anything that exists in those particular areas, that includes policies, procedures, and processes, and everything is documented. It makes life so much easier. It reduces excess conversations and noise, and it lessens confusion.

We work globally, so there are laws in different countries. We have policies on all those issues. There may be multiple people in a chain of sale, where you have a reseller or agents and you have to understand pricing or laws on tariffs or restrictions and sanctions and who you are allowed to trade with. You're still responsible so you have to train people in all these things and then refresh their understanding of that on a regular basis. That requires reissuing or referring back to the existing policy.

Q. What advice would you give others when it comes to creating policy and procedures?

Do it! It's critical for the staff to understand what they are doing, and how to do something and to have access to something because it gives the employees stability. It gives the management confidence that they don't have to babysit them. You can just point to something and say, "Here, look at this. If you have any questions, let me know. I'm happy to walk you through it," but it makes the process so simple.

Q. Is anyone in your organization able to recommend or suggest policy or changes to policy?

Oh yes, I've written a few myself, and they go on the approval channels. We have legal and all kinds of people throughout the organization who do that. I have specific procedures and things that I've piloted, and once the test is proven workable, I'll document those.

CASE STUDY #2: Michael Estey, CEO Brand Network

Q. Tell us how you use knowledge.

If I was advising my younger self, I'd say, "Don't do anything, not one single task, without it being recorded, without it being written down. Don't lift your finger, don't type a sentence, don't adjust a bit in ads, and don't make a graphic unless you are talking to the screen while doing it so that you record it and put it on file for someone else to learn what you do."

I'd also quickly get more organized as soon as possible, with enough delegation or staff to be able to have systems down, to carry out all those [functions] and to carry out more expansion. I should've pushed way harder on new products and expansion. I got content with my sales so many times, and if I just would've written down the procedures, hired the personnel, and delegated the duties, I know we would be bigger now. Because I'm one person, that's part of the problem. I was only one person holding all these hats and doing all these jobs, and I'm only as scalable as my time. I can only have twenty-four hours a day, and I need to sleep. So, if I would've written down the procedures, delegated, and just done more in that way, I would've been organized. I would've been triple what I am now.

To be successful, you have to be able to teach what you know and have it followed exactly. There's no other way to do it. You have to have a large library of policies and SOPs (standard operating procedures).

CASE STUDY #3: John Nesbit, CEO Customer Factory, approximately 30 employees

Q. Tell us how you use knowledge.

I believe it is the absolute difference between growth and no growth or struggle and no growth. Actually, having written procedures allowed me to be out of the business for almost two years and just run it with a little pinky at a distance. I had written procedures, and all that stuff was in place.

I'm very dedicated to written procedures. It's even to the point now where I'm not the only one who writes them. I used to write company policy, and then I took another jump up when I allowed all my division heads to create a divisional directive, which is a policy for their area. And I'll tell you, some of these I've never read because my executives created them for their areas to make those areas run smoother. How do they do all these little different things in the call area? I don't know. I just know the big stuff. I know that the more policies we have, the smoother the place runs.

I love writing policy; it's the magical part of the founder role. You're matching up your imagination with how you want things in the real world. And by writing it down, you'll really clarify purposes and goals and things to make it happen. I could walk into an area and solve the problems in that area, but I couldn't necessarily tell you what I did to solve them. But if I have to write the policy for someone else to follow to solve the problem, it's really much clearer. There's no substitute for that. Then you train people on the policies, and you get an increase in efficiency. It's almost an infinite level increase in efficiency, because if you don't have company policy, you can't really get anything more done than what you can verbally tell people nearby. When you get somebody new, how in the world do you get that person to have ten years of accumulated knowledge of your business when it's day one for them? You think you want to wait ten years for them to get up to speed? No, having written policy gives them all the benefit and all that learning and knowledge right now, so you can have them up to speed within days or weeks instead of never.

Q. What was your business like before you started documenting and sharing policies and procedures?

It was me desperately hanging on a raft, like at the end of *Titanic*. It was a challenge, because there was no coordination, or there was only coordination to the degree that I could keep it in my head. You're telling people, "Don't forget this. Remember to do that." It was inherently limited. When you operate like that, you have to have really smart people on the other end who can think for themselves.

Policy is all about taking my wisdom and whatever insight I have gathered and enshrining it so it can be used. I don't want to be on my deathbed saying, "Tell them to not forget to do the …" It's like a life insurance policy for your business. I consider it the most valuable part of my company.

Q. What difference did it make?

A few years ago, it was me and one other person. Now, it's me and almost two dozen. So, there's a difference. I was doing all the jobs. Now I wear the Executive Director hat and the Founder Hat. And that's it. Most days, I don't have to deliver. I don't sell. Occasionally, I'll have to do a marketing job or something like that.

It's allowed me to have a lifestyle that's more than just a growing business and money or whatever. It allowed me to take time off. I needed to be out of the business for almost two years, and it was even over the COVID times. The business was able to go along just fine with me only having limited input because all that knowledge is there; it's been written up and it's followed. Letting my executives create their own policy and procedures allowed them to keep their areas doing well. They weren't waiting for me to approve everything. That was a huge breakthrough right there, allowing people to do that. Because now I have complete write-ups on how every division operates, written by the people who were operating them when it was doing its best. So, if things go down, we just go back and reinvestigate that information. And it's right there. It's all written, so there's no guessing.

Q. How long did this take you, or how much time do you think you've spent on implementing it?

I started with one brave policy where I literally defined my own roles—President, Executive Director and Founder. I realized that those are three different jobs and I was doing all three. So, I sat down and wrote up what the difference was. I just wrote a paragraph of what each one was and how they're different.

That was actually the first policy I issued. It was just me and one other person, a "big" organization of two! Now, I spend maybe two or three hours a week writing new policies to handle some new situation, instead of jumping in and trying to handle it. For example, I just put one out not long ago about a phishing scam that was coming out that was aimed at our company and targeting Facebook marketers. It was a very convincing email that came in a very certain way that I thought my staff might get tripped up on, so I issued a policy on that right away.

I don't explain it thirty-two times. I explain it once in writing, and everybody gets it, and they study at their own speed. We have a new salesperson; this is his third day, and he said something that was right out of one of my policies, and I thought, "He's already read that one!" I don't have to explain that part of our sales process to him. It's quite a joy to behold.

Q. What advice would you give others when it comes to creating policy and procedures?

You know more than you think. And when you start writing policy, you find out just how much that is. It's also a great chance to clarify your thoughts. I firmly believe that there are people who build businesses and people who don't build the business. What is it made of? Is it just hiring people? Anybody can hire a bunch of people. The real building of a business is taking those moments to stop and put the mental effort into writing up what is successful. That's building a business.

CASE STUDY #4: Manuel Suárez, Founder & CEO of Attention Grabbing Media (AGM), 80 employees and President of Natural Slim, 150 employees. Author of *Marketing Magic*.

Q. Tell us how you use knowledge.

That's a big deal. I'm a big proponent of training and knowledge sharing. It's important to me to give people the tools and training they need to do their job. I don't hire people based on their resumes;

I hire people based on their willingness to educate themselves and how hungry they are for knowledge. That's something that's most important to me. Some of my top people here have worked with me for a long time. Some of them make six figures a year. They did not have a marketing education. They had a willingness and a hunger for more. I hired a person in the Philippines who applied to be a customer service rep. He had been a chef before, making $40 a week at a full-time job. He makes a lot of money now, and it's because he had a hunger for knowledge. He wanted to learn things. That's my process–I hire by attitude and then train them to produce.

CASE STUDY #5: Selwyn Duijvestijn, CEO, DGB Group, approximately 101 employees

Q. Tell us how you use knowledge.

Our policies and SOPs (Standard Operating Procedures) were more random in the beginning, there was more luck involved in finding the right one. At one point there were several google docs of the same procedure. Everyone had their own version of it. Now it's more aligned. And we keep doing that more and more. As we do that, it becomes simpler.

Q. Did you notice any difference in terms of business growth?

Yeah. It's like everytime we organize more, you notice it quite rapidly in the business and making sure that you have a clear policy or procedure is really good.

It becomes much more simple. Even the most complex tasks or the weirdest of situations, when broken down into steps, are able to be tackled. You just go from 1 to 2, and from 2 to 3, 3 to 4, and no matter how complex, or how long the tasks will take, it provides clarity and becomes very doable by anyone on the Team.

The results are great, so now, every time something is going wrong, we say, "Okay, let's create a policy," and then we get the person involved to read it. It works the other way around too–when something's going really well, we write it down and make it policy.

Q. How long did it take for you to start documenting and sharing the knowledge with your Team?

We used Google Docs when we started because it was easy. But once we started updating and the Team grew, it became more difficult to maintain. Now knowledge is a lot more shareable, editable, and easier to access with MetaPulse. So, we're writing more and more down.

Q. What advice would you give others when it comes to creating policy and procedures?

Once you have your Team Chart, creating policy and procedures is the next thing to do. You hear about entrepreneurs being overworked—there's so many things coming at you, especially when everything is going wrong. That's just being disorganized. If you actually write down and standardize the process by creating policy and procedures, the simpler it becomes. Then with every step of the structure you put in, you can assign that responsibility to someone, and they know what to do and you now longer have to do it.

Managers Set Objectives to Align Team Power

Have you ever played tug-o-war? The strongest Team is not always the one that wins. It's the Team that works in harmony, with *everyone pulling in the same direction.*

And that is true of any endeavor.

How many games have been lost by the so-called unbeatable team with the "star" player? Plenty!

While individual skill can be a tremendous advantage, winning consistently requires a True Team of aligned individuals. Alignment comes from having a very clear objective.

When Google was an unknown business, investor John Doer saw the potential of "online search" and became an early investor. But he did more than provide the Google founders, Larry Page and Sergey Brin, with money. He taught them the concept of <u>o</u>bjectives and <u>k</u>ey <u>r</u>esults, often referred to as OKRs.

Here's what Larry Page, co-founder of Google, had to say about OKRs:

OKRs have helped lead us to 10x growth, many times over. They've helped make our crazily bold mission of "organizing the world's information" perhaps even achievable. They've kept me and the rest of the company on time and on track when it mattered the most.

To be clear, OKRs comprise an objective (a clearly defined goal) and one or more key results (specific measures used to track the achievement of that goal).

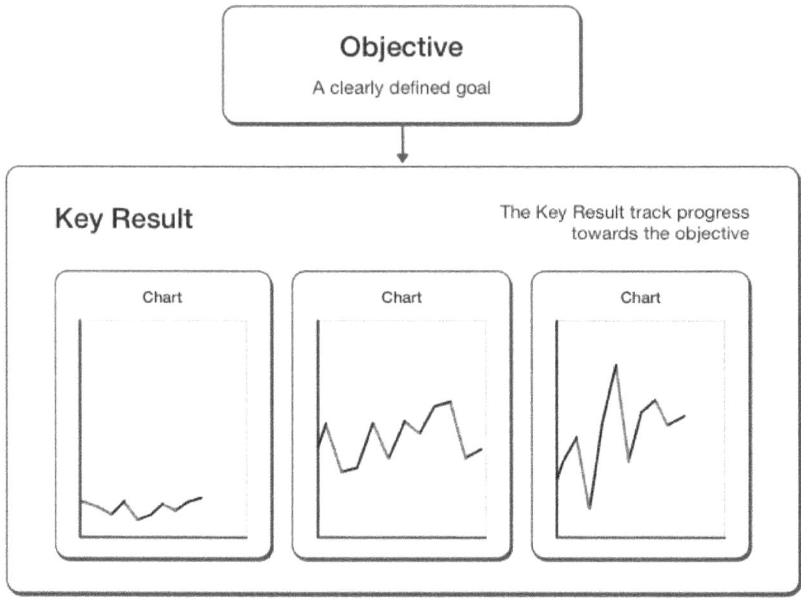

Once your Team is actively measuring and monitoring key results (that is applying Building Blocks 3 and 4), then setting objectives is the next step. When done right, this can send your business into the stratosphere.

Objectives are commonly set over a quarterly or annual basis. Setting a revenue goal for the quarter is a simple example. Such an objective has a ripple effect for the entire Team. Let's say the objective is to make $10 million in sales for the coming quarter. What resources will it take to achieve that? It requires more than just sales; it requires marketing too. It may also require new personnel, training, events, improved delivery, and so on. Every player on the Team needs to work toward that objective, and they do that by breaking down the big objective into smaller ones that they can accomplish from their zone of responsibility, from their position on the Team Chart.

It's the owner or CEO's job to set broad objectives. Two or three per quarter is enough—four at the most. Depending on the size of your Team, a few broad objectives can extrapolate into hundreds as it cascades down the Team Chart.

True Power

Imagine, as a manager, being able to see the progress of all objectives you've set and the ability to drill down into the details to see what areas of your global organization are running into difficulty. Imagine again what a Team member, lower on the Team Chart, would feel when they know they contributed to the overall objective for the quarter and helped make it happen. Finally, imagine a Team all working towards that one objective for an entire quarter, and together, they managed to pull it off. Wouldn't you love to be a part of such a True Team?

When you combine all the efforts of your Team, it generates an unstoppable force that can overcome any obstacle. That creates power.

Avoid the Opinion Trap

Just like key results, an objective is something that can easily be measured and not based on opinions. For example, the objective "improve our branding" is not easily measurable because the "improvement" is based purely on people's opinions—some may like the new branding and consider it "improved," and others may not.

One can usually find the actual objective by asking *why* such an objective is needed. "Why do we need to improve our branding?" and the answer is likely to be, "To improve sales conversions." Good, that can be measured. So the objective becomes "increase sales conversion to 30%," and part of the objective includes rebranding, but it will also include retraining the sales Team, surveying potential customers, and a whole host of other activities. Each one is a *measurable* objective and the key results of each are simple to figure out.

Monitoring such a thing may appear daunting, but not with MetaPulse. We've built the system to make setting and managing your objectives easy.

Case Studies

Client case studies on this Building Block are included at the end of the next chapter.

Objective Progress Is Measured by Key Results

As many successful people will confirm, goal setting is vital to success.

But goal setting, although vital, is not enough.

How do you know if you are making progress towards your goals?

The beauty of the OKR system is that it forces you to quantify your objectives. Progress on $10M sales for the quarter can be easily figured out. If we're halfway through the quarter, then we should have at least $5M in sales. If not, we know we're falling behind.

Progress & Risk

The purpose of a key result is to measure progress of an objective. And when measured against time, it provides a measure of *risk*.

Using the example above, if the objective is $10M in sales for the quarter and we're at $5M halfway through the quarter, we're on track and all is well. But if sales are only $1M halfway through the quarter, we're *at risk* of not making the objective. Something drastic needs to happen. The Team better be saying, "Oh no, the ship is sinking! Man all stations. Get to work!"

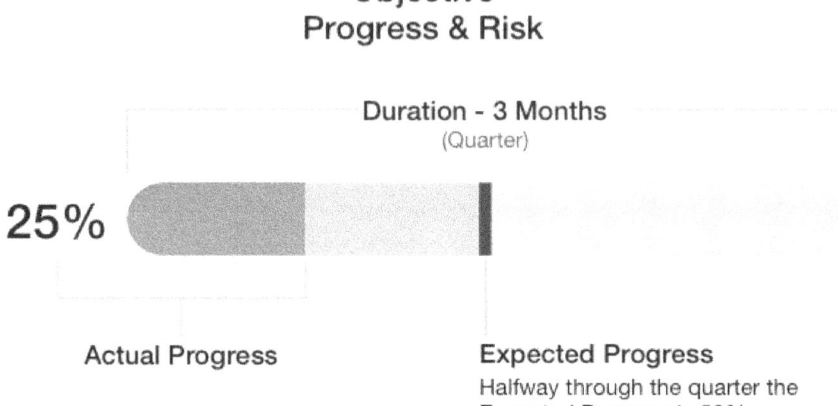

Measuring and monitoring risk creates urgency. Staying on track is key to achieving one's goals, and MetaPulse makes this possible.

Finding the Weakest Link

When using Team-centric objectives and monitoring progress and risk, it's easy to find the areas of your organization that are at risk. The illustration below provides a great example. Overall, the organization is falling behind, and we can see the Promotion and Sales Teams are in trouble.

Management needs to investigate and issue knowledge to remedy the situation and to help those Teams succeed.

Case Studies

We asked several clients who had successfully implemented Building Blocks 6 & 7 about the challenges they faced and what difference it made to their business. Here's what they had to say.

CASE STUDY #1: Company Name Withheld, approximately 1,800 employees

Q. Tell us how you use objectives.

We set it up so every person plays a part. They all have their own objectives and key results. Whether it be a financial target, or some other initiative, it's tied in with something, so they always support each other.

As an example, anyone can create an objective that aligns with another in somebody else's department. You can link it to that chain of objectives and put something in there that has to do with that, because I can see it. It makes coordination completely seamless. You don't need 50 meetings to do it. You can see, "Oh so and so is doing that, and I have something that could really help with that."

It gives clarity and focus to a lot of areas and understanding of what other people are working on. Instead of singular-mindedness, it gives you a broader view.

CASE STUDY #2 : Michael Estey, CEO Brand Network, approximately 100 employees

Q. What difference has objectives made?

What I find is often, the company and the staff are not playing a game, and they're not aligned to the goals of Q1 or Q2 or the month or the week. It's definitely a big thing for all the staff to be aligned towards the same purpose, towards the same goal, towards the same targets, and everybody's pushing each other to hit that. Everybody is playing the same game, but it's the top-level management that has to do their part so that it trickles down to everyone. I think it's a struggle when those in top-level management don't know what they want.

It's important to take the time to figure out what the goal is. Objectives help you figure that out.

CASE STUDY #3: Manuel Suárez, Founder & CEO of Attention Grabbing Media (AGM), 80 employees and President of Natural Slim, 150 employees. Author of *Marketing Magic*.

Q. Tell us how you use objectives.

We do forecasts at the beginning of the year, in the first week of January. We work out what we want to accomplish based on what we accomplished last year and what we believe the momentum should get us to. At Natural Slim, we've constantly exceeded it. That company went from 1 million to 4 to 10 to 12 to 20 to 40, and this year, it is set to do 80 million. It's incredible. I can tell you that the 80 million was not projected. Our goal was to go from 40 to 50, which was aggressive growth when you get to those levels. We have an incredible team of people, and our YouTube channel is booming. It has all come together for massive growth.

Players Record Significant Events So They Know What Worked and What Didn't

Bob Dylan said it best, "Time's they are a changin.'"
Change is the one thing we can be certain of.

A change in a promotional campaign, a change of leadership, a change in pricing—all these things can affect how the game is played.

But is it possible to know the results of such changes?

It's only with hindsight that we can look back and know if such a change was good or bad, or had no effect at all.

And that is why every player should record significant events.

Recording events provides management with a powerful tool. Results can be assessed and compared to past changes.

Let's say the sales results slowly dwindled for six months. What changed six months ago? We look over the events and ah… we see a change in pricing, or maybe it was a new promotional campaign, or perhaps the new Sales Manager hired at that time or an old Sales Manager was let go. Whatever the reason, by making note of significant events, we can see the correlation with results.

Players and managers don't need the skills of Sherlock Holmes to deduce why things are getting better or worse. They simply need all players to record significant events so they know what worked and what didn't.

Creating a culture of recording significant events can save you countless time and money and keep you on the road to success. This is a very easy Building Block to implement, so get your Team started today and you can start for free in MetaPulse.com.

Case Studies

We asked several clients who had successfully implemented this Building Block about the challenges they faced and the difference it made to their business. Here's what they had to say.

CASE STUDY #1: Company Name Withheld, approximately 1,800 employees

Q. Tell us how you use Events.

I monitor various things, so I use Events frequently. I'm a firm believer in documentation. The more you do it, the more areas you have to rely on, rather than trying to remember everything.

Without event tracking, you'd have to come up with another place to track it, or manually do it, but Events in MetaPulse is really convenient, even for me where I track notes on various things. I can go back and see what happened here, whether it be a steep rise in an area or a decline, I can see what happened there without having to rediscover it or go searching endlessly.

Q. What challenges did you face implementing Events?

I think when you see the benefit and are concerned about an area, it comes quickly. But across the entire company, it takes a little while to groove in something new. But it was so easy with only a couple of reminders and nothing major.

Q. What benefits resulted from recording significant events?

The more information you have documented about certain events, you have a much better and more accurate assessment of something at any given time. You can look at it and take action based on actual information, not a feeble attempt to guess or try to remember what happened.

CASE STUDY #2: John Nesbit, CEO Customer Factory, approximately 30 employees

Q. Tell us how you use Events?

We used this not long ago when I was looking into a downside period. We use it for data analysis to figure out what the heck was going on back then.

It tells you what knowledge items were issued and the comings and goings on the Team Chart, because otherwise, you forget and lose track. Now six months later, I can see why we suddenly got an increase in sales. We know what happened.

And that'll be in there forever.

I just added this last week. For each division head, there's the division log event where they're supposed to put any changes of note, big or small, into that little log just as a general thing, and I keep a general company one. We'll add more as they come along. I'll see what shows up in those logs and see if any of these will be actually listed as their own event.

Otherwise, trying to figure out what was happening six months ago, you have to look through weird places to find old emails just to get clues about what was going on. Now we just look Events in MetaPulse. It is so much easier.

Players Need to Alert Managers of the Good and the Bad

As a business grows, the owners and managers become less connected to the "playing field." They deal with clients less, if at all. If the business expands to multiple locations, it becomes impossible for them to know exactly what is going on every day.

Measuring and monitoring results, as discussed in Building Blocks 2 and 3, makes it possible for managers to make informed decisions and to know how well the Team is doing. However, the players at the grassroots level, those on the field, are privy to vital information much faster than any manager.

As an example, let's say a salesperson in a remote office is upsetting clients and creating problems. This will show up in the results eventually, but should the fellow Team members just ignore it and wait for management to recognise the issue? No. Management needs to know now, today, immediately.

But how can a True Team player notify management? Who do they notify?

That's the purpose of Alerts.

It's every player's role to alert management to optimum and non-optimum situations.

Just like a Formula One driver needs to know if there is a crash ahead, or if the car is not working properly, the managers need to know about potential roadblocks or disasters.

Alerting managers to such things is not something people are inclined to do, especially when it involves their co-workers or friends. Many don't like to point out other people's flaws or mistakes. However, by pointing them out, by bringing them to another's attention, they can then be addressed. Maybe the person in question needs more training (more knowledge), or perhaps there's a personal issue affecting their work, or maybe they just don't know it is their responsibility to do something! It could also be a flaw in a software program, a process, or a system. Whatever the reason, it's the duty of every player to let management know. To do otherwise is to invite disaster on the entire Team. The motto of a True Team is "Help the Team, then help the individual."

Pointing out non-optimum conduct gives management the chance to help the individual become a True Team member. If that person fails to correct or improve their results, they're a spectator, not a player.

On the flip side, it's also every player's duty to point out the things that improve results. If a Team player has done an outstanding job or if a hidden gem of know-how is suddenly uncovered, management needs to know about those things too.

Alerts then can be about the good or bad, it matters not. What matters most is that those with the power to do something should know about it as soon as possible, so they can improve the results for the entire Team. This is a culture that needs to be nurtured by the owners and senior managers. An army of alert players is what it takes to navigate the tumultuous seas of business growth.

Case Studies

We asked several clients who had successfully implemented this Building Block about the challenges they faced and the difference it made to their business. Here's what they had to say.

CASE STUDY #1: Company Name Withheld, approximately 1,800 employees

Q. Tell us how you use Alerts?

Before we used Alerts, we had to rely on somebody going out of their way to note something or to mention it. Now it's streamlined, and it helps with growth, as the less time you have to spend trying to find out about those types of activities, the more focus you can give on reviewing the information and fixing it.

I think transparency has been really critical in allowing people to understand what is happening at any given time or place, and understanding the policies gives somebody an ability to be proactive in any particular position, and it allows management to step in when needed and take some sort of action.

Q. How did you encourage the Team to use Alerts?

It's a campaign that we've been putting in over an extended period of time, and it's still something you have to remind people to do. When somebody is not doing something correctly, or in a weird way, you want to get that isolated and resolved. But you have to have somebody who is monitoring [the Alerts] and taking care of them. If you don't do that, why bother? You need somebody who is interested and responsible for Alerts to really take advantage of it.

Q. What advice would you give to others regarding implementing Alerts?

You have to have somebody there to monitor the alerts, and then you have to create an understanding of what the alerts are, what they are for, and the benefits. Like anything else in an organization, you run an internal campaign to popularize it and show how helpful it is, as opposed to the idea that you're getting someone in trouble.

CASE STUDY #2: John Nesbit, CEO Customer Factory, approximately 30 employees

Q. Tell us how you use Alerts?

My HR person checks them every day. We have service alerts and other types of alerts. I recall one we had, a sales guy was using his cell phone to make sales calls which is not per our policy, he's supposed to use our phone system so we can track the results, so things like that get picked up, and we can fix it fast.

Q. How did you encourage the Team to use Alerts?

We created the right culture for it. We have a policy that explains the alert system and explains that no one will be demoted or fired as a result of creating an alert.

I made it clear that it's the Team that keeps things correct and running smoothly. I can't do it from my role across the entire Team. I can't just yell at everybody to be good. So we've created a system that makes it routine and not a threatening thing. It's not calling the cops on somebody. It simply points out where there's a problem that needs to be handled. And I think everybody in our company knows that it takes a lot to get fired here. I'll be honest, it probably takes too much to get fired here. Because I believe in training; we try to hire really great people and then train, train, train, train. If someone makes a mistake, I assume it's a training problem or something else going on. And the second time, I assume it's still a training problem, and then the third time, I assume it has to do with the way we're administering the training. Only if someone totally proves me wrong do I reluctantly look at firing the person, but it's very rare.

Players & Managers Work in Harmony

This is not a Building Block you need to implement. Rather, it's the result of diligently implementing all prior 9 Building Blocks into a strong triangle of operational harmony.

Nevertheless, it's worth noting, because if you have upset, confusing, declining results or any kind of disharmony, then you know one or more of the Building Blocks are missing, and you don't have a True Team.

A True Team is capable of improving any dire situation and overcoming any apparent insurmountable challenge. Therefore, at the first sign of trouble, review the 9 Building Blocks. Are all the players following the Blueprint of a True Team? Are there any that can be improved?

If they are following the True Team Blueprint, then huddle together and set objectives to overcome the situation *as a Team*. If they aren't following the blueprint, take fast action to get the missing Building Blocks followed and implemented as your first objective.

Coordination

Meetings are vital in business, but often, without the True Team Blueprint in place, they can become cumbersome, ineffective, long, and a complete waste of time.

Sports teams huddle together regularly and rapidly. They discuss strategy and results. That is how meetings should be run. The purpose of a meeting is coordination and alignment. You want to ensure everyone is pulling in the same direction, and you do that by reviewing objectives and key results.

Here's the how a True Team conducts a meeting focusing on their objectives:

1. Review the progress of top-level objectives and the key results of the company.
2. Any manager with an objective at risk needs to have a plan ready to remedy the situation. The meeting is not the place to formulate the plan; it's where the plan is shared.
3. Define expected results to be achieved before the next scheduled meeting.
4. Keep all discussions to the above.
5. Keep it short, sharp, and to the point. Don't go off onto long-winded conversations between specific players. Keep the whole Team involved.

Meetings help maintain harmony, and following the method above keeps everyone focused on the main goal and builds a True Team of winners.

As we say in our business, "A quick meeting is a good meeting!"

Remember, business is a game. Games are fun, and playing with a True Team is the most fun game of all.

Join the Growth League

Whenever we share the True Team Blueprint, people are inspired by its simplicity. They get enthusiastic about the possibilities. But let's face it, despite its simplicity, implementing all 9 Building Blocks above can be tough. We know because we've done it many times ourselves.

That's why we created the Growth League.

It's a game you can play that helps you systematically implement all 9 Building Blocks. It's a game that your entire Team can participate in and become a True Team and grow your business.

The winner is the business that grows the most over each round. We measure the growth rate, relative to the business size, so it doesn't matter how big or small your business is—you can play and win.

Each round, we'll reward the winner of the Growth League with prizes and cash.

We're building a community of resources to help you implement the True Team Blueprint. In essence, we've already started building your True Team. All you need to do is join.

For full details on how to play, visit <u>metapulse.com/play</u>.

And we'll help make your business a game, where every player wins!

About the Authors

Mikel Lindsaar

At 10 years old, Mikel was fortunate enough to get his first computer, an IBM XT that dimmed the power lights when it turned on. A year later, he was using the internet (then AARNET) back before "online" was a thing. While it was all still text on a screen, he boldly told his step-father that one day, people would buy cars and houses using the internet. Despite his claim being met with scorn, he knew the world was going to be connected and he was going to be part of that.

Over the years, Mikel learnt the magic of being able to create software to solve problems, and after finding the Ruby programming language, he wrote the Mail software library that has since been downloaded over 470 million times.

After a decade of volunteering, where he learned how to build and motivate strong teams with very little, Mikel started his first company, Reinteractive. Over the last decade, he has launched 6 more companies and successfully sold 4 of them.

He created MetaPulse because he needed a system to grow his own businesses, and he realised that he had the skills and desire to build the world's first Growth Management System (GMS) to help companies around the world do the same.

Now calling Sydney, Australia, home, he is a proud father, husband, volunteer, and business owner speaking at events and helping people all over the world.

Tony Melvin

Born in the UK in 1973, Tony Melvin grew up with a passion for business. He founded his first "enterprise" around the age of 10 years old: a car washing business. His younger sister Catherine and friend Julia were the hired help. Tony was the salesman. Despite the business having only one client and lasting only a single day, he never forgot how easy it was to make money solving people's problems.

Since then, Tony has learned the ropes of business and finance from his studies and experience. Over the past 20 years, he has travelled Australia and Asia teaching finance and business principles to thousands. As managing director, he helped build the fastest-growing accounting firm in Australia, and during that same period, he co-authored three best-selling finance books.

While Tony is a successful businessman and investor, he considers himself first and foremost an educator. Considered by many an authority on finance matters, Tony is regularly interviewed and quoted in the press. As a result, Tony is a sought-after speaker.

Become a
MetaPulse Affiliate Today!

The MetaPulse affiliate program allows you to get paid for promoting MetaPulse to your audience—whether that's through email, on your blog or during a podcast or Youtube videos.

You'll make a 30% *recurring commission* for every person who signs up for MetaPulse through your unique link. And that's for the life of the customer. So long as they're paying us and you are part of our Affiliate Program, we'll pay you!

Our affiliate program offers a ton of earning potential that, since its recurring, is consistent and scalable over time.

And don't forget, MetaPulse is a *Growth Management System*. Once a business understands and starts using MetaPulse they will grow, which means they will need more users and that means your commission will grow too.

To find out more scan the QR code or go to:

MetaPulse.com/affiliates